CONTEMPORARY SUBJECT HEADINGS FOR URBAN AFFAIRS

CONTEMPORARY SUBJECT HEADINGS FOR URBAN AFFAIRS

Compiled by Greenwood Press
for the Urban Documents Program

GREENWOOD PRESS
WESTPORT, CONNECTICUT
LONDON, ENGLAND

Library of Congress Cataloging in Publication Data
Main entry under title:

Contemporary subject headings for urban affairs.

  Subject authority list for Index to current urban
documents.
  1. Subject headings—Cities and towns. 2. Subject
headings—Municipal government. I. Greenwood Press.
Z697.M8C66 1983   025.4'930776   82-25504
ISBN 0-313-23869-3 (lib. bdg.)

Library of Congress Catalog Card Number: 82-25504
ISBN: 0-313-23869-3

First published in 1983

Greenwood Press
A division of Congressional Information Service, Inc.
88 Post Road West
Westport, Connecticut 06881

Printed in the United States of America

10 9 8 7 6 5 4 3 2 1

CONTENTS

INTRODUCTION

Contemporary Subject Headings for Urban Affairs was primarily developed to provide the editors of the *Index to Current Urban Documents* (see page ix) with a precise and consistent indexing tool. Its workable vocabulary of approximately 2,700 terms was organized to conform with the requirements of the computer system used to prepare the Index. The subject authority list has been published to

- provide subscribers with a check list of all the terms that may be used to index the documents they need for a reference search.

- supply librarians and researchers with a ready-made list of terms that they may use to index their own collections of documents in related fields.

- serve as the basis for a Selective Dissemination of Information (S.D.I.) system, under which a research worker may check the terms describing his interests and ultimately obtain material indexed under those terms.

The *Index to Current Urban Documents* was first published in 1972. As the only continuing guide to the reports and other publications of local governments throughout the United States, it clearly required its own indexing vocabulary. A subject authority list was developed and throughout the years it has been revised as needed and new terms have been added to keep it current.

The vocabulary in its present form consists of a list of main terms, many of which are followed by a dash, and then a subdivision of the main terms, as in **Air pollution—research**. The advantage is that material on all aspects of a subject is place in close proximity. Theoretically, some subdivision terms, such as bibliographies, organization charts, statistics, etc., can be used under many of the main terms; however, the use of these subdivision terms has been limited to subject areas where they are most needed.

Term inversion is used to group various forms of an entity. This is indicated by a comma following a main term, as in **Courts, county; Courts, municipal; Courts, state** and **Courts, traffic.**

To avoid semantic quibbles, a number of terms combine two nearly synonymous ideas. **Administration, management; —economic aspects, impact; —inventories, surveys** are some examples.

In many cases, terms which describe one main subject are also used for breakdowns of another main subject. Education, and its subdivisions, is the main concern of reports from boards and departments of education. On the other hand, it is just one aspect of the work of agencies charged with care for the aged. Thus, we have **Education; Education—finance; Education— research**, etc., where **Education** is the main term. We also have **Aged— education**, where **education** is used as a subdivision term. This kind of double use is indicated by the note: (also used under various headings).

Scope notes are used to clarify the meaning of the terms as used in the Index. Comprehensive (master) plans, for example, is defined as "overall plans covering community facilities, housing, land use, transportation." The term is not used to describe master plans for one particular project, such as a playground or a sports stadium.

Because of the main term and subdivision design of the Index vocabulary, aspects of a subject are kept together alphabetically. See also references are therefore supplied only between related terms that are alphabetically remote. **County planning**, for example, is immediately followed by **County planning—agencies and authorities**, and see also references are therefore not used. On the other hand, see also references are supplied between **County planning** and **Metropolitan area planning**, since the two terms refer to related subjects, but are separated alphabetically.

The reference (see also specific headings), is used with terms for which the specific headings are fairly obvious and would be too numerous to list. Under Schools, for example, this reference indicates that related material may be found under headings such as **Junior high, middle schools; Summer schools; Trade and technical schools**, etc.

As users of government documents know, the subject matter covered, and the roles and interests of the issuing agencies, change with the passage of time. Because the vocabulary used to index such materials must grow and change to provide an accurate and useful key to their contents, the subject authority list for the *Index to Current Urban Documents* will be updated periodically.

URBAN DOCUMENTS PROGRAM

Description of Program

The Urban Documents Program consists of the *Index to Current Urban Documents* and the *Urban Documents Microfiche Collection*, which makes available most of the documents listed in the *Index*. It is the only such program specifically devoted to local government publications in the United States.

Acquisition

Most of the material covered by the Program is collected in cooperation with public and academic libraries from all over the country. Many local government agencies also contribute their reports on a regular basis and, in addition, specific documents are requested by the editors from other agencies. In exchange for their cooperation, the contributors are entitled to certain benefits.

Overview and Organization

The Program covers annually between 3,000 and 4,000 documents, reports and studies from city and county governments and from regional planning agencies with local government representation. Also included are publications issued by authorities, school districts and other special districts, and quasi-governmental agencies and civic organizations involved in local government research and community services. The *Index* is divided into two sections: Geographic Index and Subject Index, and it provides access to the documents by location and issuing agency, and by subject matter and type of document.

CONTEMPORARY SUBJECT HEADINGS FOR URBAN AFFAIRS

SUBJECT HEADINGS

Abortion

Abortion—law and legislation

Absenteeism, tardiness

   see also Leave of absence

Accidents

Accidents—prevention

Accidents—statistics

Accidents, building construction

   see also Occupational safety and health

Accidents, home

Accidents, industrial

   see also Occupational safety and health

Accidents, traffic

Accidents, traffic—prevention

Accidents, traffic—statistics

Accountability

Accounting methods

Achievement—tests, examinations

Acoustics

Administration, management
(also used under various programs and agencies)

Administration, management—audit reports

Administration, management—centralization, decentralization

> see also Municipal government—centralization, decentralization

Administration, management—codes, ordinances

Administration, management—handbooks, manuals

Administration, management—organization

> see also Bylaws
> Infrastructure

Adoption

> see also Children—institutional care
> Foster care

Adult education

Adult entertainment

Advertising

Affirmative action, equal opportunities programs
(also used under various programs and agencies)

Aged

Aged—bibliographies

Aged—education

Aged—employment

Aged—health programs

> see also Geriatric programs

Aged—health services

Aged—housing

Aged—income

Aged—institutional care

Aged—insurance

Aged—pensions, retirement plans

Aged—recreation

Aged—social services

> see also Geriatric programs

Aged—statistics

Aged—transportation

Aged—volunteer work

Agriculture

Aid to dependent children programs

Air conditioning

Air pollution

Air pollution—bibliographies

Air pollution—economic aspects, impact

Air pollution—environmental impact

Air pollution—law and legislation

Air pollution—research

Air pollution control

Air pollution control—agencies, authorities

Air quality

Air quality—monitoring

Air rights

Air traffic

Air traffic—regulation

Air traffic control

Air transportation

Air transportation—statistics

Air travel—statistics

Aircraft

Air-ground transport

Airlines

Airlines—regulation

Airports

Airports—administration, management

Airports—economic aspects, impact

Airports—environmental impact

Airports—facilities

Airports—finance

Airports—planning

Airports—zoning

Alcohol abuse

Alcohol abuse—education, prevention

Alcoholic beverage control

Alcoholic beverages

Alcoholic beverages—licenses

Alcoholic beverages—taxation

Alcoholics

Alcoholics—rehabilitation, treatment

Alcoholism

Alcoholism—education, prevention

Alimony

Ambulances

American Indians
SEE Native Americans

Amusement areas

see also Recreation areas

Animals, pets

see also Birds
Insects
Rodents
Wildlife

Animals, pets—codes, ordinances

Annexation

see also Municipal incorporation

Apartment houses

see also Landlord and tenant
Rental housing

Apartment houses—designs and plans

Apartment houses—social aspects, impact

Apartments

Apartments, accessory

Apportionment, reapportionment

Appraisal

Apprenticeship programs

Aquariums

Aquatic life
   SEE Marine life

Arbitration

Arboretums
   SEE Botanical gardens, arboretums

Archaeology

Architects

Architectural features

Architecture

   see also Building construction and technology

Architecture—bibliographies

Architecture—designs and plans

   see also Apartment houses—designs and plans
            Auditoriums—acoustics
            Housing—designs and plans
            School buildings—acoustics

Architecture—history

Architecture—inventories, surveys

Architecture—standards and specifications

Archives

   see also Libraries
            Records—administration, management

Arenas, stadia

Armories

Arrest

Arrest—statistics

> see also Courts—statistics
>   Crime—statistics

Arson

Art, crafts

Art commissions

Artists

Associations, organizations

Auction

Audio-visual aids

Auditoriums

> see also Civic centers

Auditoriums—acoustics

Authorities
(also used under specific headings)

> see also Special districts

Authorities—finance

Bail

Ballots

> see also Elections
>   Voting

Bankruptcy

Bankruptcy, municipal

Banks and banking
(see also specific headings)

Banks and banking—regulation

Banks and banking—taxation

Beaches

> see also Waterfront development

Beautification

Better business bureaus

  see also Consumer protection

Bibliographies
(also used under specific headings)

Bicentennial centers

Bicentennial programs

Bicentennial programs—agencies, authorities

Bicycling

Bids, bidding

  see also Contracts

Bikelanes

Bikeways

  see also Trails

Birds

Birth control

Birth rates

Births—statistics

Black Americans

Blight

Blighted areas

  see also Ghettos
          Slums
          Urban renewal

Blocks

Blood banks

Boards, commissions

Boating

  see also Marinas

Bonds

  see also County bonds
          Municipal bonds
          State bonds

Bonds—law and legislation

Bonds—taxation

Bonds, general obligation

Bonds, revenue

Bonds, serial

Bonds, sinking fund

Bonds, special assessment

Botanical gardens, arboretums

Botany

Boundaries

Boundaries, county

Boundaries, municipal

Bridges

Bridges—special districts

Bridges—standards and specifications

Bridges, toll

Bridle paths

   see also Trails

Budget

Budget—appropriations

Budget—handbooks, manuals

Budget—procedure

Budget, capital

Budget, county

Budget, county—appropriations

Budget, county, capital

Budget, county, operating

Budget, metropolitan

Budget, municipal

Budget, municipal—appropriations

Budget, municipal, capital

Budget, municipal, operating

Budget, operating

Budget, school districts

Budget, school systems

Budget, special districts

Budget, supplementary

Budget bureaus

Budget messages

Building

   see also Architecture

Building—agencies, authorities

Building—agencies, authorities—periodic reports

Building—contracts

   see also Housing—contracts

Building—standards and specifications

   see also Architecture—standards and specifica-
          tions
         Housing—standards and specifications

Building—statistics

Building, housing codes

Building, housing codes—administration, management

Building, housing codes—enforcement

Building, housing codes—inspection

Building, housing codes—inspection—statistics

Building and loan associations

Building and occupancy permits

Building and occupancy permits—statistics

Building conditions

   see also Pests
        Property improvement

Building construction and technology

see also Architecture
Prefabricated construction

Building costs

Building equipment

Building industry

see also Housing industry

Building industry—affirmative action, equal opportunities programs

Building materials

Building materials—standards and specifications

Building re-use

Building trades

Buildings

see also Apartment houses
Historic buildings
Industrial buildings
Multi-use complexes
Non-conforming structures
Office buildings
Public buildings

Buildings—condemnation

see also Housing—condemnation

Buildings—conditions

Buildings—height and bulk

Buildings—inventories, surveys

Buildings—preservation, rehabilitation

Buildings, abandoned

Buildings, high-rise

Built-up areas

Burglar alarms

Burglary

Bus and rail systems

Bus lines

Bus terminals

Buses

Business

    see also **Corporations**
            Government and business
            Industry
            Monopolies
            Retail trade
            Small business
            Trade

Business—bibliographies

Business—conferences, seminars

Business—directories

Business—inventories, surveys

Business—licenses

Business—regulation

Business—statistics

Business—taxation

Business cycles

Business districts

    see also **Central business districts**
            Commercial strips
            Industrial districts
            Shopping centers, malls

Business districts—rehabilitation

Business districts—rehabilitation—business participation

Business ethics

Business incentives

Business location

Business machines

Business organizations

Business subsidies

    see also **Government aid to business**

Bylaws

>   see also Administration, management—organi-
>   zation

CATV (cable television)

CATV (cable television)—licenses

CATV (cable television)—regulation

CETA

Canals

>   see also Waterways

Capital improvements programs

Capital improvements projects

Capital punishment

Car pools, van pools

Career development

>   see also Apprenticeship programs
>   In-service training
>   Vocational guidance

Career education

Cash management

Cemeteries

>   see also Crematories

Censorship

Census

Census—business

Census—housing

Census—minority groups

Census—population

Census—religious groups

Census tracts

Central business districts

Central business districts—rehabilitation

Central business districts—rehabilitation—business participation

Central city

    see also Inner city areas

Chambers of commerce

Charter commissions

Charters

Charters—revision

Child abuse

Child care

Child care—costs

Child guidance clinics

Child health

Child labor

Child study

Child support

Child welfare

    see also Aid to dependent children programs
            Day care services
            Foster care

Childbirth
    SEE Pregnancy and childbirth

Children

Children—institutional care

Children, emotionally disturbed

Children, gifted

Children, gifted—education

Children, handicapped

    see also Remedial education programs

Children, mentally handicapped

    see also Remedial education programs

Children, socially handicapped

>   see also Remedial education programs

Chronically ill

Chronically ill—institutional care

Churches, synagogues

Churches, synagogues—taxation

Circuit courts

Cities, towns

>   see also Metropolitan areas

Cities, towns—growth

>   see also Annexation
>   Fringe areas
>   Subdivision

Cities, towns—history

Cities, towns—statistics

Citizen, community participation
(also used under specific headings)

>   see also Volunteer work

Citizen, community participation—handbooks, manuals

City clerks

City councils

City councils—proceedings

City-county consolidation

>   see also Metropolitan government

City directories

City halls

City managers

City maps
SEE Maps, mapping

City planning

>   see also Community development
>   Metropolitan area planning
>   Neighborhood planning

City planning—administration, management

City planning—agencies, authorities

City planning—agencies, authorities—periodic reports

City planning—automation

City planning—bibliographies

City planning—business participation

City planning—citizen, community participation

City planning—directories

City planning—economic aspects, impact

City planning—finance

City planning—finance, federal aid

City planning—finance, revenue sharing, federal

City planning—finance, revenue sharing, state

City planning—finance, state aid

City planning—glossaries

City planning—handbooks, manuals

City planning—law and legislation

City planning—policy, goals

City planning—reports

City planning—research

City planning—social aspects

City planning—study and teaching

City planning—surveys

Civic centers

   see also Auditoriums

Civic organizations

Civil defense

   see also Disaster services

Civil disorders

Civil law

Civil liberties, rights

Civil procedure

> see also Judicial review
> > Probate law and practice

Civil procedure—forms

Civil service

Civil service—affirmative action, equal opportunities programs

Civil service—pensions, retirement plans

Civil service—tests, examinations

Civil service commissions

Civil service commissions—periodic reports

Climate

> see also Weather

Clinics

> see also Child guidance clinics
> > Health centers
> > School clinics

Clubs, social

Coal

Coastal zone management

Coastal zones

Code enforcement
(**—enforcement** used also under specific codes)

Codes
   SEE Ordinances, codes

Coeducation

Collective bargaining

> see also Trade agreements

Commerce
   SEE Trade

Commercial strips

Commodity exchanges

Common law

Communicable diseases

   see also Quarantine

Communicable diseases—prevention

   see also Vaccination

Communicable diseases—statistics

Communication media

Communication systems

   see also Police communications

Community centers

   see also Civic centers
          Ethnic centers

Community centers—directories

Community councils

Community development

   see also Economic development
          Industrial development
          Model cities
          Neighborhood planning

Community development—bibliographies

Community development—business participation

Community development—citizen, community participation

Community development—directories

Community development—finance

Community development—finance, federal aid

Community development—finance, revenue sharing, federal

Community development—finance, revenue sharing, state

Community development—finance, state aid

Community development—handbooks, manuals

Community development—policy, goals

Community development agencies, departments

**Community development agencies, departments—
periodic reports**

Community facilities

Community facilities—directories

Community facilities—inventories, surveys

Community facilities—planning

Community facilities—standards and specifications

Community organizations

Community organizations—directories

Community organizations—handbooks, manuals

Community structure

Community vegetable gardens

Commuters

Commuting

Complaints

> see also Ombudsmen

Comprehensive (master) plans
(overall plans covering community facilities, housing,
land use, transportation)

Concessions, privileges

> see also Parks—concessions

Condominium housing

Condominiums

Conferences
SEE Conventions, convention facilities

Conservation
SEE Resource management

Constitutions

Constitutions—state

Construction loans

> see also Mortgage finance

Consultants

Consultants—directories

Consultants reports

Consumer education

Consumer movement

Consumer price index

Consumer protection

Consumer protection agencies

    see also Better business bureaus

Consumer protection agencies—periodic reports

Consumer services

Consumers

Consumers—surveys

Container systems

Contract compliance

Contracts

    see also Bids, bidding
             Labor contracts, agreements
             Leases

Contracts—conflict of interest

Conventions, convention facilities

Cooperative associations

Cooperative housing

Cooperative housing—taxation

Cooperative research

Cooperative stores

Coroners

Corporation counsels

Corporation law

Corporations

    see also Government corporations

Corporations—finance

Corporations—taxation

Correctional facilities

> see also Juvenile detention homes
> Prisons
> Reformatories, juvenile

Corrections departments

Corrections departments—periodic reports

Corruption

Corruption, political

> see also Government—unethical and corrupt
> practices

Cost analyses

Cost and standard of living

> see also Consumer price index
> Income

Cost/benefit analyses

Council-manager plan

> see also Manager plan
> Mayor-council plan

Councils of government
SEE Regional planning—agencies, councils of
government

Counties

Counties—consolidation

> see also City-county consolidation

Counties—growth

Counties—history

Counties—statistics

County attorneys

County bonds

County clerks

County debt

County employees
(see also subdivisions following **Public employees**)

County executives, officials

County executives, officials—directories

County expenditures

County finance

see also Budget, county
Metropolitan government—finance

County finance—accounting

County finance—audit reports

County government

see also Intergovernmental cooperation, relations
Metropolitan government

County government—automation

County government—bibliographies

County government—centralization, decentralization

County government—citizen, community participation

County government—community planning

County government—consolidated reports

County government—costs

County government—directories

County government—handbooks, manuals

County government—interdepartmental cooperation, relations

County government—law and legislation

County government—organization

County government—organization charts

County government—periodic reports

County government—policy, goals

County government—proceedings

County government—public relations

County government—reorganization

County government—statistics

County managers

County master plans
  SEE Comprehensive (master) plans

County-municipal cooperation, relations

  see also City-county consolidation

County planning

  see also Comprehensive (master) plans
    Metropolitan area planning

County planning—agencies, authorities

County planning—agencies, authorities—periodic reports

County planning—citizen, community participation

County planning—finance

County planning—law and legislation

County planning—policy, goals

County planning—research

County revenues

County services

County services—costs

County services—inventories, surveys

County services—planning

Court reform

Courthouses

Courts

Courts—fines

Courts—reporting

Courts—statistics

Courts, county

Courts, municipal

Courts, state

Courts, traffic

Credit

> see also Installment finance
> Interest rates
> Mortgage finance

Credit cards

Credit unions

Crematories

> see also Cemeteries

Crime
(see also specific headings)

> see also Victims of crime
> Violations

Crime—causes

Crime—costs

Crime—detection

> see also Coroners

Crime—prevention

> see also Prisoners—rehabilitation

Crime—prevention—citizen, community participation

Crime—reports

> see also Uniform crime reporting

Crime—research

Crime—statistics

> see also Arrest—statistics
> Courts—statistics

Criminal codes

Criminal evidence

Criminal identification

Criminal justice

Criminal law

Criminal procedure

   see also Trials

Criminals

   see also Prisoners

Criminals—rehabilitation

Criminals—restitution

Crowd, riot control

Cultural activities

   see also Performing arts

DOT

Dams

   see also Irrigation

Day care services

Day care services—licenses

Death rates

Deaths—statistics

   see also Mortality—causes

Deeds

   see also Land titles

Demographic data

Demographic studies

Demolition

   see also Buildings—condemnation
              Housing—demolition

Demonstration reports

   see also Model cities

Dental services

Dentistry—regulation

Depleted areas

   see also Ecological studies
           Natural resources

Design control

Detectives

Developers

   see also Real estate business

Development

Development—citizen, community participation

Development—controls

Development—cost/benefit analyses

Development—economic aspects, impact

Development—environmental impact

Development—policy, goals

Development corporations

Developments

   see also Housing developments

Diplomats

Directories
(also used under specific headings)

Disaster assistance

Disaster hazard areas

   see also Flood plains

Disaster preparedness

Disaster services

   see also Civil defense
           Emergency housing
           Emergency medical services

Disasters

Disasters—reconstruction

Discrimination

Diseases

> see also Chronically ill
> Communicable diseases
> Mental illness
> Toxicological hazards

Diseases—statistics

Displacement

> see also Relocation

District attorneys

> see also County attorneys

District courts

Divorce
SEE Marriage and divorce

Documentation

Documents
SEE Public documents

> see also Electronic data processing
> Information systems

Domestic abuse, violence

Drainage

> see also Flood control
> Sewerage and sewage disposal

Drivers

Drivers—licenses

Driveways

Dropouts

Drug abuse

Drug abuse—bibliographies

Drug abuse—education, prevention

Drug addicts

Drug addicts—rehabilitation, treatment

> see also Halfway houses

Drugs

Earthquakes

> see also **Civil defense**
> **Disaster preparedness**

Ecological studies

> see also **Depleted areas**
> **Natural resources**

Ecology

Economic base studies

Economic conditions

Economic conditions—projections

Economic conditions—statistics

Economic development

> see also **Industrial development**

Economic development—agencies, authorities

Economic development—agencies, authorities—periodic reports

Economic development planning

Economic models

Economic opportunity

> see also **Government regulation of business**

Economic policy

Economic research

Economics

Education
(see also specific headings)

Education—accountability

Education—bibliographies

Education—citizen, community participation

Education—costs

Education—directories

Education—finance

Education—finance, federal aid

Education—finance, state aid

Education—glossaries

Education—handbooks, manuals

Education—law and legislation

Education—planning

Education—policy, goals

Education—research

Education—state supervision

Education—statistics

    see also Schools—statistics

Education—surveys

Education, bilingual

Education departments

Education departments—periodic reports

Education programs

    see also Remedial education programs

Educational attainment

    see also Dropouts

Educational facilities

    see also School buildings
            Universities and colleges—facilities

Educational facilities—planning

Educational guidance

Educational parks

Election boards

Election districts

    see also Legislatures—apportionment, reappor-
        tionment

Elections

    see also Nominations
           Recalls
           Referenda

Elections—costs

Elections—law and legislation

Elections—reforms

Elections—registration

Elections—returns

Elections—statistics

Elections, conduct of

Elections, contested

Elections, primary

Elections, special

Electric apparatus and appliances

Electric apparatus and appliances—standards and
  specifications

Electric power

Electric power, nuclear

Electric power, nuclear—environmental impact

Electric transmission

Electric utilities

   see also Public utilities

Electric utilities—agencies, authorities

Electric utilities—agencies, authorities—periodic
  reports

Electric utilities—environmental impact

Electric utilities—facilities

Electric utilities—finance

Electric utilities—franchises

Electric utilities—management

Electric utilities—planning

Electric utilities—rates

Electric utilities—regulation

Electric utilities—statistics

Electrical codes

Electronic data processing

> **see also Information systems**

Electronic data processing—agencies, departments

Elementary schools
  SEE Primary schools

Elevators

Emergency housing

Emergency medical services

Emergency medical services, ambulances

Emergency planning

Emergency services

Eminent domain

Employee benefits

Employee handbooks, manuals

Employee performance standards

Employee productivity

Employee savings plans

Employee training

> **see also In-service training**

Employees

Employees—salaries, wages

Employees—surveys

Employment
  (also used under specific headings)

> **see also Labor supply**
>   **Unemployment**

Employment—inventories, surveys

Employment—projections

Employment—statistics

Employment, supplementary

Employment agencies

Employment counseling

   see also Vocational guidance

Employment programs

Energy audits

Energy conservation

Energy consumption

Energy recovery

Energy resources
(see also specific headings)

**Engineering
SEE Technology**

Engineers

Enterprise zones

Environmental design

Environmental health

Environmental impact
(also used under specific headings)

Environmental impact statements

Environmental management

Environmental protection

Environmental protection—agencies, authorities

**Environmental protection—agencies, authorities—
periodic reports**

**Environmental protection—economic aspects, im-
pact**

Environmental protection—law and legislation

Environmental quality

Environmental quality—bibliography

Epidemics

Equal employment opportunities

Erosion

Estate tax

Ethnic centers

Ethnic groups
   SEE Population—ethnic groups

Evacuation

Eviction

Exceptional children,
   SEE Remedial education programs

Excess profits tax

Excise tax

Ex-convicts—employment

Executors, public

Exhibitions, exhibition halls

Explosives

Express streets and freeways

Factories

Factory inspection

Family

   see also Marriage and divorce

Family allowance

   see also Guaranteed annual income
            Negative income tax
            Public assistance

Family courts

Family income and expenditures

   see also Cost and standard of living

Family income and expenditures—housing

Family planning services

Family welfare

   see also Child welfare

Farms, farming

Feasibility studies

Federal aid
(also used under specific headings)

Federal contracts

Federal-county relations

Federal government

Federal-municipal relations

Federal reserve banks

Federal-state relations

Ferries

Finance
(also used under specific headings)

Finance—intergovernmental relations

Finance—legislation

Finance—legislative control

Finance—research

Finance departments

Finance departments—audit reports

Finance departments—periodic reports

Fire—causes

Fire—statistics

Fire alarms

Fire departments

Fire departments—emergency medical services

Fire departments—organization charts

Fire departments—periodic reports

Fire escapes

Fire fighting equipment, methods

Fire houses

Fire losses—statistics

Fire prevention

Fire prevention—inspection

Fire prevention—law and legislation

Fire prevention—safety devices and measures

Fire prevention—statistics

Fire protection

Fire protection—outside services

Fire protection—statistics

Firemen

Firemen—handbooks, manuals

Firemen—pensions, retirement plans

Firemen—salaries, wages

Firemen—training

Fireworks

Fiscal year

Fish, seafood

Fisheries, fishing

    see also Hunting, fishing

Flood control

    see also Dams
           Rivers

Flood plains

Flood plains—zoning

Floods

    see also Disaster services
           Insurance, flood

Food allowance

Food banks

Food distribution

Food handling

Food industry

Food inspection

Food programs

Food stamps

Food supply

Foreign trade zones

Forests

Foster care

   see also Adoption
            Children—institutional care

Foundations, charitable and educational

Foundations, charitable and educational—directories

Four-day week

   see also Hours of labor

Franchise tax

Franchises

Freight terminals

   see also Materials handling

Freight transportation

Fringe areas

   see also Cities, towns—growth
            Suburbs

Fringe benefits

Fuel

Fuel, fossil

Fuel, synthetic

Fuel storage

Gambling, legalized

Gambling, legalized—periodic reports

Garages

   see also Municipal garages

Garages—designs and plans

Garden cities

Gardening, gardens

Gas, natural

Gas apparatus and appliances

Gas apparatus and appliances—standards and specifications

Gas utilities

see also Public utilities

Gas utilities—agencies, authorities

Gas utilities—agencies, authorities—periodic reports

Gas utilities—environmental impact

Gas utilities—finance

Gas utilities—franchises

Gas utilities—management

Gas utilities—rates

Gas utilities—regulation

Gasoline
  SEE Petroleum

Gasoline service stations

Gasoline service stations—regulation

Gasoline tax

Gazeteers

Geologic data

Geologic factors

Geology

Geothermal energy

Geriatric programs

see also Aged—health programs
         Aged—health services
         Aged—social services

Ghettos

see also Blighted areas
         Slums
         Urban renewal

Gift tax

Glossaries
(also used under specific headings)

Golf courses

Government

Government—accountability

Government—bibliographies

Government—unethical and corrupt practices

　　see also Contracts—conflict of interest
　　　　　Corruption, political

Government aid to business

　　see also Business subsidies

Government and business

Government corporations

Government liability

Government loans

　　see also Intergovernmental loans

Government regulation of business

Government research

　　see also Municipal reference libraries

Government research—contracts and specifications

Governors

Governors' messages

Grade crossings

Grand juries

Grant applications

Grants-in-aid

　　see also Land grants

Guaranteed annual income

　　see also Family allowance
　　　　　Negative income tax
　　　　　Public assistance

Guidebooks

> **see also Street guides**

Gun control

> **see also Weapons**

HEW

HUD

Halfway houses

Handbooks, manuals
(also used under specific headings)

Handicapped

> **see also Aged**
> > **Children, handicapped**
> > **Children, mentally handicapped**
> > **Mentally handicapped**

Handicapped—care and treatment

Handicapped—education

Handicapped—employment

Handicapped—grants-in-aid

Handicapped—housing

Handicapped—institutional care

Handicapped—rehabilitation

Handicapped—transportation

> **see also Aged—transportation**

Hazardous materials, waste

Headstart programs

Health

> **see also Communicable diseases**
> > **Diseases**
> > **Hospitals**
> > **Nursing homes**

Health—agencies, authorities

Health—agencies, authorities—periodic reports

Health—bibliographies

Health—codes, ordinances

Health—glossaries

Health—law and legislation

Health—statistics

Health care

   see also Aged—health programs

Health care, home

Health care practitioners

Health care practitioners, paraprofessional

Health care practitioners, professional

   see also Physicians, general practice
            Physicians, surgeons
            Nurses

Health centers

Health departments

Health departments—organization charts

Health departments—periodic reports

Health districts

Health districts—finance

Health education

Health examinations

Health examinations—statistics

Health facilities

   see also Clinics
            Hospitals
            Nursing homes
            School clinics

Health facilities—directories

Health facilities—inventories, surveys

Health facilities—planning

Health hazards

Health maintenance organizations

Health maintenance organizations—rates

Health maintenance programs

Health maintenance programs—finance

Health manpower

Health planning

Health planning—agencies, authorities

Health planning—agencies, authorities—periodic reports

Health planning—handbooks, manuals

Health planning—policy, goals

Health research

Health services

> **see also Dental services**
> **Family planning services**
> **Hospital services**
> **Medical services**
> **Mental health services**

Health services—costs

Health services—directories

Health services—finance

Health services—inventories, surveys

Health services—law and legislation

Health services—monitoring

Health services—policy, goals

Health services—statistics

Heating

Heating—codes, ordinances

Heating, central

Heating, district

Heating plants

Helicopters

High risk areas
  SEE Disaster hazard areas

High schools

Hispanic Americans

Historic buildings

Historic buildings—designation

Historic buildings—inventories, surveys

Historic buildings—preservation, restoration

Historic districts

Historic districts—designation

Historic sites

Historic sites—designation

Historic sites—preservation, restoration

Historical commissions

Historical societies

Home economics

   see also Household equipment

Home improvement
  SEE Property improvement

Home ownership

   see also Mortgage finance

Home rule

Homicide

Hospices

Hospices—services

Hospital services

Hospital services—costs

Hospital services—group plan

   see also Medical services—group plan

Hospital services—statistics

Hospitals

> see also Clinics
>> Health centers
>> Nursing homes
>> Prison hospitals

Hospitals—administration, management

Hospitals—agencies, authorities

Hospitals—agencies, authorities—periodic reports

Hospitals—costs

Hospitals—directories

Hospitals—finance

Hospitals—inventories, surveys

Hospitals—monitoring

Hospitals—planning

Hotels, motels

Hotels, motels—regulation

Hours of labor

> see also Four-day week

Household equipment

> see also Electric apparatus and appliances
>> Gas apparatus and appliances

Households

Households—expenditures

Households—expenditures—housing

Households—income

Housing
(see also specific headings as
Apartment houses
Minority groups—housing
Public housing etc.)

Housing—agencies, authorities

Housing—agencies, authorities—periodic reports

Housing—associations, organizations

Housing—bibliographies

Housing—codes, ordinances

Housing—codes, ordinances—enforcement

Housing—condemnation

    see also Building conditions

Housing—congestion

Housing—contracts

Housing—costs

Housing—demolition

Housing—density

Housing—designs and plans

Housing—directories

Housing—economic aspects, impact

Housing—equipment

    see also Air conditioning
            Heating
            Plumbing

Housing—finance

Housing—finance, federal aid

Housing—finance, state aid

Housing—glossaries

Housing—inspection

Housing—inventories, surveys

Housing—land acquisition

Housing—law and legislation

Housing—location, sites

Housing—maintenance, management

Housing—planning

Housing—policy, goals

Housing—preservation, rehabilitation

Housing—preservation, rehabilitation—finance

Housing—projections

Housing—security

Housing—social aspects, impact

Housing—standards and specifications

    see also Building—standards and specifications

Housing—statistics

    see also Building and occupancy permits—sta-
            tistics
          Census—housing
          Public housing—statistics

Housing—taxation

Housing, substandard

Housing, substandard—statistics

Housing, temporary

Housing and health

Housing conditions

Housing developments

Housing industry

Housing market

Housing market analyses

Housing programs

Housing programs, federal

Housing programs, municipal

Housing programs, state

Housing research

Housing research contracts

Housing re-use

Housing starts

Housing stock

Housing stock—inventories, surveys

Housing subsidies

Human relations

Human services

Human services—directories

Human services—glossaries

Human services—handbooks, manuals

Human services—inventories, surveys

Hunting, fishing

Hunting, fishing—licenses

Hunting, fishing—statistics

Hydroelectric power

Hydrofoils

Hydrology

    see also Flood control
            Oceanography
            Water resources

Illiteracy

Immigrants

Immunization

Impeachment

Income

    see also Family income and expenditures
            Guaranteed annual income
            Households—income

Income—statistics

Income—surveys

Income, personal

Income, personal—statistics

Income tax

Income tax, corporate

Income tax, municipal

Incorporation

Indian reservations

Indictment

see also Grand juries

Industrial buildings

see also Factories

Industrial capacity

Industrial development

see also Economic development

Industrial districts

Industrial location

see also Site selection

Industrial parks

Industrial research

Industrial waste, wastewater

Industry
(see also subdivisions following
Business)

see also Government aid to business

Industry—administration, management

Industry—automation

Industry—bibliographies

Industry—directories

Industry—environmental impact

Industry—inventories, surveys

Industry—law and legislation

Industry—statistics

Infant mortality

Infant mortality—statistics

Inflation

Inflation—government control

    see also Price regulation

Inflation—impact

Information resources

Information services

Information systems

    see also Documentation

Infrastructure

Inheritance tax

Injunctions

    see also Labor injunctions

Inner city areas

    see also Central city

Insecticides

Insects

Insects—control

In-service training

Installment finance

    see also Retail trade

Insulation

Insurance

    see also Social security
              Workmen's compensation

Insurance—law and legislation

Insurance—statistics

Insurance—taxation

Insurance, accident

Insurance, automobile

Insurance, automobile, no-fault

Insurance, county

Insurance, disability

Insurance, fire

Insurance, flood

Insurance, group

> see also Hospital services—group plan
> Medical services—group plan

Insurance, health

Insurance, health—law and legislation

Insurance, income protection

Insurance, liability

> see also Workmen's compensation

Insurance, life

Insurance, life—rates

Insurance, malpractice

Insurance, municipal

Insurance, property

Insurance, state

Insurance, survivors'

Insurance, tornado

Insurance, unemployment

Insurance companies

Integration, racial

> see also Affirmative action, equal opportunities
> programs
> Race relations
> Schools—discrimination, integration

Intelligence—tests, examinations

Interdepartmental cooperation, relations

Interest rates

Intergovernmental loans

Intergovernmental cooperation, relations
(see also other headings as
County-municipal cooperation, relations)

Intermunicipal cooperation, relations

    see also Municipal leagues

International organizations

Interstate cooperation, relations

Inventories
(see also specific headings)

Investigating commissions

Investments

    see also Bonds
            Securities
            Stocks

Irrigation

Judges

Judges—salaries, wages

Judicial councils

Judicial decisions

Judicial districts

Judicial procedure

    see also Criminal procedure
            Prosecution
            Sentence
            Trials

Judicial review

Judiciary, powers of

Junior high, middle schools

Junk yards

Juries

    see also Grand juries

Justice, administration of

    see also Courts
            Law enforcement
            Legal assistance

Justices of the peace

Juvenile courts

Juvenile courts—statistics

Juvenile delinquency

see also Child guidance clinics
Reformatories, juvenile

Juvenile delinquency—statistics

Juvenile delinquents—rehabilitation

Juvenile detention homes

see also Reformatories, juvenile

Kindergartens

Kindergartens—statistics

LEAA

Labeling

Labor

see also Child labor
Trade unions
Working conditions
Workmen's compensation

Labor—bibliographies

Labor—costs

Labor—law and legislation

Labor—regulation

Labor—statistics

Labor contracts, agreements

see also Collective bargaining

Labor injunctions

Labor productivity

Labor relations

see also Collective bargaining

Labor standards

see also Hours of labor
Work measurement
Working conditions

Labor supply

> **see also Apprenticeship programs**
> **Employment**
> **Manpower programs**

Labor supply—projections

Labor supply—statistics

Lakes

Land

> **see also Open space land**
> **Public lands**
> **Real property**
> **Vacant land**

Land acquisition
(also used under various projects)

> **see also Eminent domain**

Land banks

Land grants

Land management

Land resources

> **see also Open space land**
> **Public lands**
> **Vacant land**

Land titles

> **see also Leases**
> **Real property**

Land use

Land use—classification

Land use—cost/benefit analyses

Land use—environmental impact

Land use—history

Land use—inventories, surveys

Land use—law and legislation

Land use—policy, goals

Land use—statistics

Landfill

Landlord and tenant

> **see also Leases**
> **Rent control**

Landmarks

> **see also Historic buildings**
> **Monuments**

Landmarks—designation

Landmarks—inventories, surveys

Landmarks—preservation, restoration

Landscape architecture

Landslides

Law and legislation
(also used under specific headings)

Law departments, municipal

Law enforcement

> **see also Criminal law**
> **Police**

Law enforcement—administration, management

Law enforcement—agencies, authorities

Law enforcement—bibliographies

Law enforcement—citizen, community participation

Law enforcement—directories

Law enforcement—facilities and equipment

Law enforcement—finance

Law enforcement—finance, federal aid

Law enforcement—finance, state aid

Law enforcement—law and legislation

Law enforcement—organization

Law enforcement—planning

Law enforcement—statistics

Law enforcement methods

Law practice

Law suits

Lawyers

League of Women Voters

Learning disabilities
SEE Remedial education programs

Leased housing
SEE Rental housing

Leases

see also Landlord and tenant

Leave of absence

see also Maternity leave
Sabbatical year
Sick leave

Legal assistance

Legal ethics

Legal notice

Legal research

Legislative indexes

Legislative procedures

Legislative procedures—handbooks, manuals

Legislative sessions

Legislatures

see also City councils

Legislatures—apportionment, reapportionment

Leisure

see also Recreation

Libraries

see also Municipal reference libraries
Planning libraries
School libraries

Libraries—administration, management

Libraries—automation

Libraries—directories

Libraries—inventories, surveys

Libraries—periodic reports

Libraries—planning

Libraries—standards and specifications

Libraries—statistics

Libraries, county

Libraries, regional

Libraries, state

Library acquisition lists

Library buildings

Library catalogs

Library extension services

Library resources

Licenses, professional

Licenses and permits

    **see also Building and occupancy permits
Business—licenses**

Licenses and permits—ordinances

Licenses and permits—statistics

Light rail systems

Lighting

    see also Street lighting

Littering

Living conditions

Lobbying

Lobbying organizations

    see also Pressure groups

Local government

    see also Annexation
          County government
          Intergovernmental cooperation, relations
          Metropolitan government
          Municipal government
          Special districts

Local government—costs

Local government—finance

    see also County finance
          Metropolitan government—finance
          Municipal finance

Local government—statistics

Local government—taxation

Local housing authorities

Local housing authorities—finance

Lots, parcels

    see also Community vegetable gardens

Lotteries

Low-cost housing

Low-income housing

Loyalty investigations

    see also Public employees—loyalty investigations

Maintenance and repair

Maintenance codes

Manager plan

    see also Council-manager plan
          Mayor-council plan

Manholes

Manpower programs

    see also Apprenticeship programs

Maps, mapping

> **see also Population—maps**
> **Street guides**
> **Tax maps**

Marinas

Marine biology

Marine life

Market analyses

> **see also Economic base studies**
> **Housing market analyses**
> **Retail trade—market analyses**

Marketing

Markets

Marriage and divorce

Marriage and divorce—statistics

Martial law

Mass transportation

> **see also Buses**
> **People movers**
> **Rapid transit**
> **Street cars**
> **Subways**

Mass transportation—economic aspects, impact

Mass transportation—environmental impact

Mass transportation—finance

Mass transportation—inventories, surveys

Mass transportation—planning

Mass transportation—policy, goals

Master plans
  SEE Comprehensive (master) plans

Materials handling

> **see also Freight terminals**

Maternal and infant care, postnatal
  SEE Postnatal care

Maternal and infant care, prenatal
  SEE Prenatal care

Maternal mortality

Maternal mortality—statistics

Maternity leave

Mayor-council plan

Mayors

Mayors' messages

Medicaid, Medicare

Medical ethics

Medical practice—regulation

Medical research

Medical services

  see also Aged—health programs
          Clinics
          Geriatric programs
          Hospitals
          Mental health services

Medical services—costs

Medical services—group plan

  see also Hospital services—group plan

Medical services—policy, goals

Medical services—statistics

Medical services, private

Medical services, socialized

Medical services, state

Mental health services

  see also Halfway houses

Mental health services—statistics

Mental hygiene

Mental illness

Mental illness—statistics

Mentally handicapped
(see also subdivisions following
Handicapped)

Merit system

see also Civil service
Personnel management

Methodology

Metropolitan area planning

see also Cities, towns—growth
City planning
County planning
Regional planning
Suburbs

Metropolitan area planning—agencies, authorities

see also Regional planning—agencies, councils
of governments

Metropolitan area planning—agencies, authorities—periodic reports

Metropolitan area planning—citizen, community participation

Metropolitan area planning—law and legislation

Metropolitan area planning—policy, goals

Metropolitan area planning—research

Metropolitan area surveys

Metropolitan areas

see also Cities, towns—growth
Intergovernmental relations
Suburbs

Metropolitan government

see also County government
Intergovernmental cooperation, relations

Metropolitan government—finance

Metropolitan government—law and legislation

Metropolitan government—organization

Metropolitan government—organization charts

Middle-income housing

Middle schools
  SEE Junior high, middle schools

Migrant workers

Migrant workers—education

Migrant workers—health services

Migrant workers—housing

Migration

Military housing

Military installations

Minimum wages

> see also **Personnel management—job classifi-
>   cation, salary ranges
>   Salaries, wages**

Mining

Minority groups
  (see also specific headings)

> see also **Civil liberties
>   Integration, racial**

Minority groups—bibliographies

Minority groups—business enterprises

Minority groups—education

Minority groups—employment

> see also **Affirmative action, equal opportunities
>   programs**

Minority groups—housing

> see also **Mortgage finance—minority groups**

Mobile home parks

Mobile homes

Model cities

> see also **Community councils
>   Community development**

Model cities—audits

Model cities—citizen, community participation

Model cities—glossaries

Model cities—law and legislation

Model cities agencies, departments

Model cities agencies, departments—organization charts

Model cities agencies, departments—periodic reports

Model codes

Model houses

Model laws and ordinances

Moderate income housing

Money

    see also Banks and banking
           Credit
           Finance
           Inflation
           Prices

Monopolies

Monuments

Morbidity—statistics

Mortality—causes

Mortality—statistics

Mortgage banks

Mortgage finance

    see also Construction loans
           Savings and loan associations
           Veterans' guaranteed loans

Mortgage finance—law and legislation

Mortgage finance—minority groups

    see also Minority groups—housing

Mortgage foreclosure

Mortgage insurance

Mortgage interest rates

Mortgage market

Motor equipment and supplies, government

Motor vehicles

   see also **Buses**
           Mobile homes
           Parking
           Taxicabs

Motor vehicles—abandoned

Motor vehicles—inspection

Motor Vehicles—maintenance and repair

Motor vehicles—registration

Motor vehicles—taxation

Multi-use complexes

Municipal bonds

Municipal corporations

   see also **Charters**

Municipal debts

Municipal employees
   (see also subdivisions following
   Public employees)

Municipal expenditures

Municipal finance

   see also **Bankruptcy, municipal**
           Budget, capital
           Budget, municipal
           Capital improvements programs
           Real property—taxation
           Taxation

Municipal finance—accounting

Municipal finance—audit reports

Municipal finance—federal aid

Municipal finance—handbooks, manuals

Municipal finance—legislative control

Municipal finance—policy, goals

Municipal finance—state aid

Municipal garages

Municipal government

> **see also Administration, management
> Home rule
> Intergovernmental cooperation, rela-
> tions
> Intermunicipal cooperation, relations**

Municipal government—automation

Municipal government—bibliographies

**Municipal government—centralization, decentrali-
zation**

**Municipal government—citizen, community partic-
ipation**

Municipal government—consolidated reports

Municipal government—costs

Municipal government—directories

Municipal government—emergency powers

Municipal government—handbooks, manuals

**Municipal government—interdepartmental cooper-
ation, relations**

Municipal government—law and legislation

Municipal government—organization

> **see also Council-manager plan
> Infrastructure
> Manager plan
> Mayor-council plan**

Municipal government—organization charts

Municipal government—periodic reports

Municipal government—policy, goals

Municipal government—public relations

Municipal government—reorganization

Municipal government—statistics

Municipal incorporation

> **see also Annexation**

Municipal leagues

Municipal liability

    see also Insurance, liability

Municipal officers

Municipal officers—directories

Municipal outside services

Municipal ownership

Municipal reference libraries

Municipal reference libraries—acquisition lists

Municipal research

Municipal revenues

Municipal services

Municipal services—costs

Municipal services—directories

Municipal services—inventories, surveys

Municipal services—planning

Museums

Native Americans

    see also Indian reservations

Natural resources

    see also Ecological studies
           Energy recovery
           Energy resources
           Resource planning
           Resource recovery

Negative income tax

    see also Family allowance
           Guaranteed annual income
           Public assistance

Neighborhood analyses

Neighborhood associations

Neighborhood business areas

Neighborhood planning

Neighborhood planning—citizen, community participation

Neighborhood planning—policy, goals

Neighborhood planning—social aspects, impact

Neighborhood preservation, rehabilitation

see also Building, housing codes
Central business districts—rehabilitation
Model cities
Urban homesteading
Urban renewal

Neighborhood preservation, rehabilitation—bibliography

Neighborhood preservation, rehabilitation—citizen, community participation

Neighborhood preservation, rehabilitation—finance

Neighborhood preservation, rehabilitation—policy, goals

Neighborhoods

New towns

see also City planning
Garden cities
Planned communities

New towns in town

Newspapers

Noise

see also Airports—environmental impact

Noise—law and legislation

Noise control

Noise prevention

Nominations

see also Elections

Non-conforming structures

Non-conforming uses

Non-profit organizations

Non-profit housing organizations

Nuclear crisis

Nuclear power
  SEE Electric power, nuclear

Nuisances

  see also Animals, pets
            Insects
            Noise
            Odors
            Pests
            Rodents

Nurses

Nursing homes

  see also Aged—institutional care
            Chronically ill—institutional care
            Handicapped—institutional care

Nursing homes—directories

Nursing homes—law and legislation

Nutrition programs

Nutritionists

  see also Health care practioners, professionals

OEO

Occupational diseases

Occupational safety and health

  see also Accidents, building construction
            Accidents, industrial
            Safety programs

Occupational safety and health—law and legislation

Occupational safety standards

Occupations

  see also Vocational guidance

Oceanography

Odors

Office buildings

Office management

> see also Personnel management

Offices

Offshore drilling

Ombudsmen

> see also Complaints

Open space—land acquisition

Open space land

> see also Community vegetable gardens
>   Land use
>   Parks
>   Recreation

Open space plans

Operations research

Ordinances, codes
(see also specific headings)

Organization charts
(also used under specific headings)

Oriental Americans

Owner-built houses

PERT

Packaging—law and legislation

Parades

Paraprofessionals

Pardon

Parking

Parking—facilities

Parking—inventories, surveys

Parking—regulation

Parking, park and ride facilities

Parking fees

Parking meters

Parks

Parks—agencies, authorities

Parks—agencies, authorities—periodic reports

Parks—concessions

Parks—designs and plans

Parks—directories

Parks—finance

Parks—inventories, surveys

Parks—planning

Parkways

Parole

   see also Probation

Parole—law and legislation

Parole officers

Patents

Paving plants, municipal

Payments in lieu of taxes

Payroll tax

Peddling

Pedestrian malls

   see also Shopping centers, malls

Pedestrian traffic

Pensions, retirement plans
(also used under specific headings)

People movers

Performance audits

Performance standards

Performing arts

   see also Cultural activities

Periodicals and newsletters

Perjury

Personal property

Personal property—taxation

Personnel management

Personnel management—bibliographies

Personnel management—certification

Personnel management—eligibility

Personnel management—glossaries

Personnel management—handbooks, manuals

Personnel management—hiring practices

Personnel management—job analysis, classification

Personnel management—job classification, salary ranges

Personnel management—job description

Personnel management—law and legislation

Personnel management—policy and planning

Pesticides

Pesticides—environmental impact

Pesticides—regulation

Pests

> see also Animals, pets
> Insects
> Nuisances
> Rodents

Petroleum

Petroleum industry and trade

Petroleum industry and trade—law and legislation

Physicians, general practice

Physicians, surgeons

Physicians, surgeons—fees

Physicians, surgeons—insurance, malpractice

Physicians, surgeons—professional standards—
  monitoring

Pipelines

Pipelines—environmental impact

Pipes

  see also Plumbing
       Sewers

Pipes—standards and specifications

Plan reviews

Planetaria

Planned communities

  see also City planning
       Garden cities
       New towns

Planned communities—social effect

Planners

Planning
  (see also specific headings, as
  City planning)

Planning—administration, management

Planning—aesthetics

Planning—agencies, authorities

Planning—agencies, authorities—organization
  charts

Planning—agencies, authorities—periodic reports

Planning—awards

Planning—bibliographies

Planning—citizen, community participation

Planning—directories

Planning—finance

Planning—glossaries

Planning—handbooks, manuals

Planning—law and legislation

Planning—research

Planning, zoning boards

Planning, zoning boards—conflicts of interest

Planning libraries

Planning models

Plants, trees

Platting

Playgrounds

Plumbing

> see also Drainage
>   Pipes
>   Sewers

Plumbing—standards and specifications

Plumbing codes

Podiatry—regulation

Police

Police—affirmative action, equal opportunities programs

Police—administration, management

Police—directories

Police—emergency duty

Police—equipment

Police—handbooks, manuals

Police—interdepartmental relations

Police—manpower programs

Police—pensions, retirement plans

Police—public relations

Police—salaries, wages

Police, aerial

Police, special units

Police, traffic

> see also Accidents, traffic

Police communications

Police communications—automation

Police departments

Police departments—directories

Police departments—organization charts

Police departments—periodic reports

Police dogs

Police ethics

Police facilities

Police power

Police stations

Police women

Policemen

   see also Detectives

Policemen—training

Political advertising

Political bosses

Political campaigns

Political campaigns—finance

Political campaigns—regulation

Political conventions

Political ethics

   see also Corruption, political

Political parties

Poor

   see also Ghettos
         Poverty programs
         Public welfare
         Slums

Population

   see also Cities, towns—growth
         Demographic data

Population—age distribution

Population—density

Population—distribution

Population—economic aspects

Population—education

Population—estimates

Population—ethnic groups

Population—maps

Population—national groups

Population—policy

Population—projections

Population—racial groups

Population—religious groups

Population—sex distribution

Population—shift

Population—social aspects

Population—statistics

Population—trends

Pornography

Ports

    see also Freight terminals

Ports—agencies, authorities

Ports—agencies, authorities—finance

Ports—agencies, authorities—periodic reports

Ports—directories

Ports—regulations

Ports—statistics

Post office buildings

Postnatal care

Poverty programs

Poverty programs—citizen, community participation

Prefabricated construction

Pregnancy and childbirth

Prenatal care

Prenatal mortality

Prenatal mortality—statistics

Pressure groups

see also Lobbying

Preventive medicine
  SEE Health care

Price indexes

see also Consumer price index

Price regulation

Prices

see also Cost and standard of living
         Inflation

Primary schools

Prison hospitals

Prison labor

Prison reform

Prison schools

Prisoners

see also Ex-convicts—employment
         Pardon
         Parole

Prisoners—psychiatric care

Prisoners—rehabilitation

Prisoners—statistics

Prisons

see also Correctional facilities

Prisons—planning

Prisons—statistics

Public administration
  SEE Administration, management

Public assistance

  see also Aid to dependent children programs
            Food stamps
            Guaranteed annual income
            Rent subsidies, housing allowances

Public assistance—finance

Public assistance—statistics

Public buildings

Public buildings—auction

Public buildings—directories

Public buildings—finance

Public buildings—planning

Public defenders

Public demonstrations

Public documents

  see also Archives
            Charters
            Constitutions
            Records

Public documents—bibliographies

Public employees

  see also Civil service
            Personnel management

Public employees—affirmative action, equal opportunities programs

Public employees—benefits

Public employees—directories

Public employees—handbooks, manuals

Public employees—labor agreements

Public employees—labor negotiations

Public employees—loyalty investigations

Public employees—pensions, retirement plans

Public employees—performance standards

Public employees—political activities

Public employees—productivity

Public employees—residence requirements

Public employees—rules and regulations

Public employees—salaries, wages

Public employees—surveys

Public employees—training

see also Career development

Public employees—training, bilingual

Public entertainments

see also Parades
        Sports events
        Tournaments

**Public health nursing
SEE Health care, home**

Public hearings

Public housing
(see also subdivisions following
Housing)

see also Low-income housing
        Non-profit housing organizations
        Scatter site housing

Public housing—administration, management

Public housing—eligibility

Public housing—finance

Public housing—law and legislation

Public housing—social aspects, impact

Public housing—statistics

Public lands

see also Parks

Public lands—auction

Public lands—law and legislation

Public lands—taxation

Public liability

   see also Municipal liability

Public meetings

Public officials

   see also County executives, officials
        Municipal officers

Public officials—appointment

Public officials—directories

Public officials—salaries, wages

Public officials—tenure

Public opinion

   see also Pressure groups

Public opinion polls

   see also Surveys

Public ownership

Public property

Public relations

   see also Municipal government—public relations

Public safety

   see also Accidents—prevention
        Civil defense
        Occupational safety and health
        Safety education

Public service employment programs

Public services

Public services—costs

Public services—directories

Public services—inventories, surveys

Public services—planning

Public utilities

Public utilities—agencies, authorities

Public utilities—agencies, authorities—periodic reports

Public utilities—control

Public utilities—finance

Public utilities—ownership

Public utilities—planning

Public utilities—rates

Public utilities—regulation

Public utilities—statistics

Public utilities—taxation

Public utilities commissions

Public welfare

> see also Child welfare
> Family welfare
> Food banks
> Poor
> Social services

Public welfare—law and legislation

> see also Social legislation

Public welfare—personnel

Public welfare—statistics

Public welfare departments

Public welfare departments—organization charts

Public welfare departments—periodic reports

Public works

> see also Capital improvements programs

Public works—finance

> see also Special assessments

Public works—planning

Public works—standards and specifications

Public works departments

Public works departments—organization charts

Public works departments—periodic reports

Pumping stations

Purchasing

    see also Bids, bidding
          Contracts

Purchasing—procedures

Purchasing departments

Purchasing departments—periodic reports

Quality of life
    SEE Living conditions

Quarantine

Questionnaires

Race relations

    see also Civil liberties, rights
          Integration, racial

Race tracks

Racial groups

    see also Minority groups

Racing

    see also Gambling, legalized

Radar

Radio and television

    see also CATV (cable television)

Radio and television—ownership

Radio and television—regulation

Radio communication

    see also Police communications

Radiological hazards

    see also Toxicological hazards

Railroad equipment, rolling stock

Railroad safety devices and measures

Railroad stations

Railroad terminals

   see also Freight terminals

Railroads

Railroads—agencies, authorities

Railroads—taxation

Rape

Rape—prevention

Rape—statistics

Rapid transit

Rapid transit—finance

Rapid transit—planning

Real estate business

   see also Investments
          Leases

Real estate business—discrimination, integration

Real estate business—law and legislation

Real property

   see also Deeds
          Eminent domain
          Mortgage finance
          Subdivision

Real property—appraisals

Real property—assessments

Real property—maintenance, management

Real property—taxation

Real property, public

   see also Public buildings
          Public lands

Real property, public—auction

Real property, public—management

Recalls

Records

   see also Archives
        Report writing

Records—administration, management

Recreation

   see also Aged—recreation
        Amusement areas
        Community centers
        Land use
        Leisure
        Parks

Recreation—administration, management

Recreation—associations

Recreation—directories

Recreation—facilities

Recreation—finance

Recreation—inventories, surveys

Recreation—planning

Recreation areas

Recreation centers

Recreation departments

Recreation departments—periodic reports

Recreation programs

   see also Sports activities

Recycling of waste products
  SEE Resource recovery

Referenda

Reformatories, juvenile

Refrigeration

Refugees

Refuse and refuse disposal

    see also Resource recovery
           Salvage
           Sanitation
           Sewerage and sewage disposal
           Water pollution

Refuse and refuse disposal—agencies, authorities

Refuse and refuse disposal—agencies, authorities—periodic reports

Refuse and refuse disposal—environmental impact

Refuse and refuse disposal—facilities

Refuse and refuse disposal—finance

Refuse and refuse disposal—law and legislation

Refuse and refuse disposal—outside services

Refuse and refuse disposal—planning

Regional agencies, authorities

Regional agencies, authorities—periodic reports

Regional directories

Regional growth

Regional planning

    see also Comprehensive (master) plans
           County planning
           Metropolitan area planning
           Resource planning

Regional planning—agencies, councils of government

Regional planning—agencies, councils of government—periodic reports

Regional planning—bibliographies

Regional planning—citizen, community participation

Regional planning—directories

Regional planning—finance

Regional planning—glossaries

Regional planning—handbooks, manuals

Regional planning—inventories, surveys

Regional planning—law and legislation

Regional planning—policy, goals

Regional planning—research

Regional zoning

Rehabilitation services
(see also specific headings)

Religious activities

  see also Churches, synagogues

Religious groups

Relocation

  see also Displacement

Remedial education programs

Rent control

Rent control—law and legislation

Rent subsidies, housing allowances

Rental housing

  see also Apartment houses
          Public housing

Rents

  see also Landlord and tenant

Report writing

Reporting

  see also Style manuals
          Uniform crime reporting

Research
(also used under specific headings)

Reservoirs

Residential care facilities

Residential districts

Resource management

> **see also Natural resources**

Resource recovery

> **see also Energy recovery**

Rest rooms

Restaurants

Retail stores

> **see also Business districts**
> **Shopping centers, malls**

Retail trade
(see also subdivisions following
Business)

> **see also Installment finance**

Retail trade—law and legislation

Retail trade—market analyses

Retail trade—statistics

Retirement

> **see also Pensions, retirement plans**

Retirement plans
SEE Pensions, retirement plans

Revenue sharing

Revenue sharing, federal
(also used under specific headings)

Revenue sharing, state

Revenues

Revenues—statistics

Rezoning

Right to read programs

Riot control
SEE Crowd, riot control

Risk management

Rivers

Road departments

Road departments—periodic reports

Road signs

Road systems

Roads

    see also Express streets and freeways
            Sidewalks
            Traffic

Roads—construction

Roads—designs and plans

Roads—environmental impact

Roads—finance

Roads—finance, federal aid

Roads—finance, state aid

Roads—improvements

Roads—maintenance and repairs

    see also Streets—maintenance and repairs

Roads—maps

Roads—planning

Roads—planning—land acquisition

Roads—separation

Roads, bypass

Roads, elevated

Roads, secondary

Roads, toll

Rodents

Rooms, rooming houses

Runaways

Rural areas

SMSA

Sabbatical year

Sabotage

Safety codes

>   see also Traffic codes

Safety devices and measures

Safety education

Safety programs

Safety zones

Salaries, wages
(also used under specific headings)

Sales tax

Salvage

>   see also Refuse and refuse disposal
>   Resource recovery
>   Sewerage and sewage disposal

Sampling

Sanitary codes

Sanitary inspection

>   see also Factory inspection
>   Food inspection

Sanitation

>   see also Pests
>   Refuse and refuse disposal
>   Sewerage and sewage disposal

Sanitation departments

Sanitation departments—periodic reports

Savings and loan associations

Savings banks

Scale models

Scatter site housing

>   see also Low-income housing
>   Public housing

School administrators

School age parents—education

School attendance

    see also Dropouts
            Truancy

School attendance—statistics

School boards

School boards—proceedings

School buildings

School buildings—acoustics

School buildings—construction

School buildings—costs

School buildings—finance

School buildings—planning

School children

School children, medical examinations

School clinics

School closings

School discipline

School districts

School districts—finance

School districts—periodic reports

School libraries

School lunch programs

School systems

School systems—finance

School systems—labor agreements

School systems—labor negotiations

School systems—organization charts

School systems—periodic reports

School tuition

Schools
(see also specific headings)

Schools—administration, management

Schools—citizen, community participation

Schools—curricula

Schools—curricular materials

Schools—directories

Schools—discrimination, integration

Schools—enrollment

Schools—examination

Schools—handbooks, manuals

Schools—inventories, surveys

Schools—pupil transport

Schools—standards

Schools—statistics

Schools, private

Scientific research

Scientific societies

Scientific societies—directories

Sculpture

Securities

    see also Bonds
             Investments

Securities—law and legislation

Securities—taxation

Securities marketing

Security systems and measures

Sentence

    see also Probation

Separation of powers

Septic tanks

Service charges

   see also Payments in lieu of taxes

Sewer districts

Sewer districts—finance

Sewer districts—periodic reports

Sewerage and sewage disposal

   see also Plumbing
                Refuse and refuse disposal
                Septic tanks
                Water treatment, waste water

**Sewerage and sewage disposal—agencies, author-
ities**

**Sewerage and sewage disposal—agencies, author-
ities—periodic reports**

**Sewerage and sewage disposal—environmental
impact**

Sewerage and sewage disposal—facilities

Sewerage and sewage disposal—finance

**Sewerage and sewage disposal—law and legisla-
tion**

Sewerage and sewage disposal—planning

Sewers

   see also Drainage

Sewers—maintenance, management

Sewers—standards and specifications

Shelters

   see also Emergency planning

Sheriffs

Shipping

Shipping—statistics

Ships

Shopping centers, malls

   see also Pedestrian malls

Shorelands
  SEE Coastal zones

Shortages

Sick leave

Sickle cell anemia

Sickle cell programs

Sidewalks

   see also People movers

Sign codes

Signs, billboards

   see also Road signs
         Traffic signs

Site planning

Site selection

   see also Business location
         Industrial location

Slaughter houses

Sludge disposal

Slumlords

Slums

   see also Ghettos
         Housing, substandard
         Urban renewal

Small business

Small claims courts

Snow removal

Social change

Social conditions

Social conditions—statistics

Social groups

Social legislation

Social policy

Social problems

see also Alcoholism
        Drug abuse
        Unemployment

Social psychology

Social science research

Social Security

Social service agencies

Social service agencies—directories

Social service agencies—inventories, surveys

Social service agencies—periodic reports

Social services

see also Aged—social services
        Mental hygiene
        Public assistance
        Public welfare

Social services—bibliographies

Social services—directories

Social services—finance

Social services—glossaries

Social services—handbooks, manuals

Social services—inventories, surveys

Social services—law and legislation

Social services—planning

Social services—statistics

Social surveys

Social workers

Social workers—certification

Socio-economic analyses

Soils

Solar energy

Solid waste disposal

> **see also Refuse and refuse disposal**
> **Resource recovery**

Space considerations

Special assessments

Special districts
(see also specific headings)

> **see also Authorities**
> **Local housing authorities**

Special districts—finance

Special districts—periodic reports

Special education
SEE Remedial education programs

Sports activities

Sports events

Sports facilities

Spouse abuse
SEE Domestic abuse, violence

Standard consolidated areas

Standpipes

State aid
(also used under specific headings)

State bonds

State-county cooperation, relations

State debts

State development commissions

State government—centralization, decentralization

State government—directories

State government—emergency powers

State-municipal cooperation, relations

State officials

State ownership

State planning

State planning agencies

State supervision of local finance

State taxation

Statistics
(also used under specific headings)

Stock exchanges

    see also Commodity exchanges

Stock transfer tax

Stocks

Stockyards

Storage

Storms

    see also Disaster services
             Floods

Stormwater

Street cars

Street closing

Street guides

Street lighting

Street openings

    see also Manholes

Street widening

Streets

    see also Roads
             Sidewalks
             Traffic

Streets—finance

Streets—improvements

Streets—maintenance and repairs

Streets—planning

Streets—standards and specifications

Strikes

> see also Trade unions

Strip zoning

> see also Commercial strips

Students

> see also Universities and colleges—students

Style manuals

> see also Report writing

Subdivision

> see also Suburbs

Subdivision regulation

Subsidies

> see also Housing subsidies
> Rent subsidies, housing allowances

Subsidized housing

Suburbs

> see also Cities, towns—growth
> Metropolitan areas
> New towns

Subways

Suggestion systems

Suicide

Summer schools

Supreme courts

Survey methods

Surveying

Surveys
(also used under specific headings)

Swimming pools

Systems analysis

Tardiness
    SEE Absenteeism, tardiness

Taverns

Tax abatement

Tax auditing

Tax collection

Tax collection—statistics

Tax collection devices

Tax delinquency

Tax delinquent property

Tax departments

Tax departments—periodic reports

Tax evasion

Tax exemption

Tax fraud

Tax immunity

Tax incentives

Tax limits

Tax maps

Tax reform

Tax revenues

Tax revenues—utilization

Tax rolls

Taxation

    see also Payments in lieu of taxes
            Real property—taxation
            Special assessments

Taxation—administration, management

Taxation—assessments, equalization

Taxation—intergovernmental relations

Taxation—law and legislation

Taxation—policy, goals

Taxation, double

Taxation, indirect

Taxation, reciprocal

Taxation rates

Taxicabs, limousines

Taxicabs—regulation

Taxicabs—statistics

Taxpayers

Taxpayers—surveys

Teachers

see also Sabbatical year
        Universities and colleges—faculty

Teachers—associations

Teachers—certification

Teachers—contracts

Teachers—education

Teachers—pensions, retirement plans

Teachers—salaries, wages

Teachers—tenure

Technical assistance programs

Technology

Telephone, telegraph

see also Communication systems

Telephone companies

Telephone companies—rates

Telephone companies—regulation

Telephone directories

Telephone poles

Tenant associations

Tenants

   see also Landlord and tenant

Tenure

Terminals

   see also Airports
           Bus terminals
           Freight terminals
           Ports
           Railroad terminals

Terrorism, terrorists

Testing

Theaters

Theaters, drive-in

Tobacco tax

Topographical data

Torrens system

Torts

Tourist attractions

Tourist trade

Tourists

Tournaments

Townhouses

Toxicological hazards

   see also Insecticides
           Occupational diseases
           Pesticides
           Radiological hazards

Trade

Trade—regulation

Trade—statistics

Trade agreements

Trade and technical schools

   see also Vocational education

Trade associations

Trade unions

Trade unions—benefit plans

Traffic

> **see also Air traffic**
> **Express streets and freeways**
> **Motor vehicles**
> **Pedestrian traffic**
> **Police, traffic**
> **Safety zones**

Traffic—planning

> **see also Roads—planning**
> **Terminals**

Traffic—regulation

> **see also Parking—regulation**

Traffic codes

Traffic control

Traffic departments

Traffic departments—periodic reports

Traffic safety

> **see also Safety zones**

Traffic signals

Traffic signs

Traffic surveys

Traffic violations

Trails

> **see also Bikeways**
> **Bridle paths**

Training
(also used under specific headings)

> **see also In-service training**

Training, bilingual

Training programs

Transportation

see also Car pools, van pools
Commuting
Container systems
Mass transportation
Terminals
Traffic
Waterways

Transportation—agencies, authorities

**Transportation—agencies, authorities—organiza-
tion charts**

**Transportation—agencies, authorities—periodic re-
ports**

Transportation—automation

Transportation—bibliographies

Transportation—directories

Transportation—economic aspects, impact

Transportation—environmental impact

Transportation—equipment

Transportation—finance

Transportation—finance—accounting

Transportation—finance, federal aid

Transportation—finance, state aid

Transportation—glossaries

Transportation—inventories, surveys

Transportation—law and legislation

Transportation—planning

**Transportation—planning—citizen, community par-
ticipation**

Transportation—policy, goals

Transportation—projections

Transportation—rates

Transportation—research

Transportation—statistics

Travel—estimates

Travel—projections

Travel—statistics

Trees
SEE Plants, trees

Trials

see also Criminal procedure

Truancy

Trucks, trucking

Trusts and trustees

Tuition fees

Tunnels

UMTA

Underground structures

Unemployables

see also Handicapped—employment

Unemployment

see also Employment programs
Public service employment programs

Unemployment—statistics

Unemployment, technological

Uniform crime reporting

see also Crime—reports

Unincorporated areas

Unions
SEE Trade unions

Universities and colleges

Universities and colleges—curricula

Universities and colleges—facilities

Universities and colleges—facilities—planning

Universities and colleges—faculty

see also Sabbatical year

Universities and colleges—finance

see also Tuition fees

Universities and colleges—housing

Universities and colleges—inventories, surveys

Universities and colleges—planning

Universities and colleges—research

Universities and colleges—research facilities

Universities and colleges—research services to neighboring communities

Universities and colleges—statistics

Universities and colleges—students

Urban design

see also Beautification

Urban form

Urban homesteading

Urban observatories

Urban renewal

see also Blighted areas
        Central business districts—rehabilitation
        Model cities
        Neighborhood preservation, rehabilitation

Urban renewal—agencies, authorities

Urban renewal—agencies, authorities—organization charts

Urban renewal—agencies, authorities—periodic reports

Urban renewal—business participation

Urban renewal—citizen, community participation

Urban renewal—finance

Urban renewal—law and legislation

Urban renewal—surveys

Vacancy surveys

Vacant land

Vaccination

> **see also Communicable diseases**
> **Immunization**

Vagrants

Vandalism

Vehicular movement

Vending machines

Venereal diseases

Venereal diseases—statistics

Veterans

Veterans—education

Veterans—employment

Veterans—health services

Veterans—housing

Veterans—statistics

Veterans' guaranteed loans

Veterinary medicine

Veterinary medicine—regulation

Veto

Victims of crime

Violations

> **see also Traffic violations**

Vital statistics
(covers birth and mortality statistics; separate compilations are entered under individual headings)

Vocational education

> **see also Trade and technical schools**

Vocational guidance

> **see also Career development**

Voluntary organizations

Volunteer work

    see also Aged—volunteer work

Voters

Voting

    see also Elections

Voting machines

Wage incentives

Warehouses

Water

    see also Floods

Water conduits

Water conservation

Water consumption

Water departments

Water departments—periodic reports

Water distribution

    see also Pipelines
            Pumping stations

Water districts

Water districts—finance

Water meters

Water pollution

    see also Sewerage and sewage disposal

Water pollution—bibliographies

Water pollution—economic aspects, impact

Water pollution—environmental impact

Water pollution—glossaries

Water pollution—law and legislation

Water pollution—research

Water pollution control

Water power

Water quality

Water quality—monitoring

Water quality—standards and specifications

Water resources

> see also Dams
> > Reservoirs
> > Rivers
> > Wells

Water resources—management

Water rights

Water storage

> see also Dams
> > Reservoirs
> > Standpipes

Water supply

> see also Irrigation
> > Lakes
> > Plumbing
> > Rivers

Water supply—bibliographies

Water supply—costs

Water supply—engineering

> see also Flood control

Water supply—glossaries

Water supply—law and legislation

Water supply—standards and specifications

Water treatment

Water treatment—costs

Water treatment—facilities

Water treatment, wastewater

Water treatment, wastewater—costs

Water treatment, wastewater—facilities

Waterfront development

    see also Beaches

Watersheds

Waterways

    see also Canals
                Lakes
                Rivers

Waterworks

    see also Public utilities

Waterworks—finance

Waterworks—rates

Waterworks—regulation

Weapons

Weather

    see also Climate
                Storms

Weather reports

Weights and measures

Welfare
    SEE Public welfare

Wells

Wetlands

Wildlife

Wildlife protection

Wildlife sanctuaries

Wind energy

Witnesses

    see also Perjury

Women

Women—education

Women—employment

Women—legal status

Work measurement

Work programs

Working conditions

> **see also** Hours of labor
>   Occupational safety and health

Workmen's compensation

Yards

Youth

> **see also** Children
>   Juvenile delinquency
>   School children

Youth—employment

Youth services

Youthful offenders

Youthful offenders—rehabilitation

Zoning

> **see also** Non-conforming structures
>   Regional zoning
>   Rezoning
>   Strip zoning

Zoning—codes, ordinances

> **see also** Subdivision regulation

Zoning—hardship variances

Zoning—policy, goals

Zoning boards

> **see also** Planning, zoning boards

Zoning boards—conflict of interest

Zoning boards—periodic reports

Zoning legislation

> **see also** Subdivision regulation

Zoning maps

Zoological gardens